The Zombie Miner
of Cannock Chase

Dark Tunnels, Haunting Echoes: True Tales from Beneath
England's Strangest Forest

Lee Brickley

Copyright @ Lee Brickley 2023

Chapters:

Introduction..5

The Mining History of Cannock Chase.......................9

Mists of Brereton..17

Hednesford Hills' Haunting Hums..............................23

Littleton's Ghostly Locomotive...................................29

Cannock Wood's Phantom Footsteps........................35

The Shadows of Hawkins' Workshop.........................41

Rugeley's Resonating Remnants................................47

Castle Ring's Cryptic Chronicle..................................53

Hednesford's Bewitching Breeze................................59

Wyrley's Weeping Willow...65

Rawnsley's Radiant Lantern.......................................71

Beaudesert's Broken Ballad.......................................77

Chasetown's Chilling Charade....................................83

Norton Canes' Nostalgic Nocturne.............................89

Mill Green's Mournful Murmurs.................................95

Leacroft's Lamenting Lullaby...................................101

West Cannock No1 Colliery's Silent Pursuit............107
Shoal Hill's Silent Sentry............113
Coppice Colliery's Cautious Caress............119
Gentleshaw's Guiding Glow............125
Zombie in the Town Centre............129
Four Ashes' Fading Farewell............135
Afterword............141
About The Author............145

Introduction

As the sun's last rays retreat behind the dense treeline of Cannock Chase, casting long shadows upon its undulating landscape, I find myself returning to its embrace time and again, drawn to its mysteries and enigmatic tales. This sprawling forest, with its lush greens and tangled thickets, has been a witness to countless seasons, lives, and legends. Among the ancient trees and winding trails of England's storied woods, I've come to know many tales. But none have ensnared my investigator's curiosity and haunted my thoughts quite like the chilling legends buried deep within the heart of this very woodland.

Long before I ever stepped foot as a paranormal investigator into the depths of Cannock Chase, its history had left an indelible mark on my psyche. With every visit, every whispered story, the place seemed to beckon me with more urgency. The once-prosperous mining heritage, where undaunted miners ventured into the bowels of the earth in pursuit of coal and fortune, is more than just an industrial legacy; it's a testament to the indomitable spirit of a bygone era. However, the more I explored, the more I felt that in their quest, the miners might not just have struck coal. They might have stirred something far older, far more malevolent.

Through years of research, countless interviews, and sleepless nights spent pouring over accounts, I've curated the chilling tales contained within these pages. Tales shared by locals, each narrating their own personal, hair-raising encounters with what they're certain is the 'Zombie Miner'. Twenty-one brave individuals, each bringing forth stories that have often left me looking over my shoulder long after our conversations have ended. They speak of a figure steeped in the history of the mines, a spectral presence with eyes that echo pain and longing, skin and clothing tainted with the coal from the cavernous depths it once inhabited. And always, that unmistakable, haunting moan - as if the very land itself lamented its presence.

But what truly unifies these seemingly disparate accounts?

Is it the power of collective folklore, passed down through hushed conversations, or perhaps the eerie, almost tangible atmosphere of Cannock Chase that makes one's imagination run wild? Or, as I sometimes wonder in the quiet, shadowy hours, are these witnesses truly encountering a remnant of a dark, buried history, a spirit forever tethered to the mines and forests it once called home?

As you delve deeper into this volume, be ready to question every sound, every fleeting shadow. The boundaries between the known and the unknown blur, and with each tale, you'll find yourself oscillating between scepticism and the unnerving possibility of belief. Each rustling of the leaves, the softest of murmurs, the fleeting chill in the air – might they not be mere natural occurrences? Could they be subtle reminders of the Zombie Miner's proximity?

I invite you, dear reader, to accompany me on this most profound of journeys through the soul, history, and enigmas of Cannock Chase. Within the confines of this book, and perhaps even within your very core, you might just discover that the lines dividing truth, legend, and unsolved mysteries are far more tenuous than you ever believed.

The Mining History of Cannock Chase

Cannock Chase, spanning thousands of acres of undulating terrain, has long been a place of historical significance, beauty, and enigma. Its legacy, woven from tales of labour, innovation, and sacrifice, stands proudly in the annals of England's industrial history. While the forested landscape today is a sanctuary for nature lovers, dog walkers, and families, the scars of its mining past run deep, a testament to an era that transformed not only the landscape but also the very fabric of its community.

The origins of mining in Cannock Chase can be traced back to mediaeval times. Local land charters from the 13th century reference the extraction of coal, indicating a long-standing relationship between the people and the black gold that lay beneath their feet. This initial foray into mining was rudimentary, with coal extracted from shallow bell pits, often no deeper than 20 feet. The coal was primarily used for local purposes—blacksmithing, heating homes, and limited trade.

However, it wasn't until the 19th century, amid the fervour of the Industrial Revolution, that Cannock Chase emerged as a central hub for coal extraction. The voracious appetite for coal, driven by industrial growth, steam engines, and expanding urban centres, set the stage for a mining boom in the region. Advancements in mining technology, coupled with the construction of the local railway lines, meant that coal from Cannock Chase could be transported farther afield, fetching better prices and incentivizing deeper and more extensive mining operations.

By the mid-1800s, numerous collieries dotted the landscape, with names like 'Hawkins', 'Littleton', and 'Cannock & Rugeley' becoming synonymous with the prosperity and challenges of the coal industry. Mining villages sprouted around these collieries, as thousands of miners and their families settled in the region, seeking employment and a better future.

Life for a Cannock Chase miner was one of hard work, camaraderie, and constant danger. The typical day began before dawn, with miners descending into the bowels of the earth, equipped with pickaxes, shovels, and Davy lamps. The subterranean world they entered was a place of echoing silence, broken only by the rhythmic sounds of tools striking rock and the distant hum of machinery.

While the coal seams in Cannock Chase were rich, they were also embedded in a complex web of geological formations. Miners often had to navigate through narrow, winding tunnels, some of which were prone to sudden collapses or flooding. The ever-present danger of methane gas explosions was a constant threat, leading to many tragic incidents over the years. Yet, amidst these challenges, a strong sense of brotherhood flourished. Miners relied on one another for safety and support, forging bonds that often lasted a lifetime. Stories of heroism, where miners risked their lives to save their colleagues from mishaps, became legends in their own right, passed down through generations.

The growth of the mining industry in Cannock Chase had

profound socio-economic implications. The influx of miners led to the development of schools, churches, and community centres. However, the industry also brought its share of challenges. Strikes and labour disputes, often arising from demands for better wages and working conditions, were not uncommon. Moreover, the health implications for miners were severe. Prolonged exposure to coal dust led to respiratory illnesses, with many miners suffering from the dreaded 'black lung' disease. Despite the hardships, a sense of pride and resilience defined the mining communities. They celebrated their triumphs, mourned their losses, and faced adversities together.

By the early 20th century, Cannock Chase had firmly established itself as one of the major coal-producing regions in England. World Wars saw a surge in demand, with coal from the mines fueling warships, trains, and factories. However, the post-war era signalled the beginning of the end for the coal industry in Cannock Chase. The advent of alternative energy sources, coupled with economic factors and diminishing coal seams, led to a gradual decline. By the 1960s, many of the collieries had become unprofitable and faced closure. The last colliery in

Cannock Chase, the Littleton Colliery, closed its doors in 1993, marking the end of an era. The once-thriving mining villages faced economic challenges, with many miners having to find alternative employment.

Today, the scars of the mining era are still visible in Cannock Chase. Slag heaps, remnants of railway tracks, and dilapidated buildings serve as silent reminders of a bygone age. Yet, nature has a way of healing. Many of the old mining sites have been reclaimed by nature, with woodlands, grasslands, and lakes providing habitats for a diverse range of flora and fauna. Cannock Chase, in its present avatar, is a blend of history, natural beauty, and a spirit of resilience. Its mining legacy is not just in the relics left behind, but in the stories, memories, and soul of its people—a community shaped by the echoes from the deep.

As the sun sets over Cannock Chase, casting long shadows that merge with the darkness of the night, tales older than the woods themselves begin to emerge. Amongst the whispers of the wind and the rustling leaves, a more sinister story has carved its niche in the lore of the region. As if the very earth that bore witness to countless miners' sweat, toil, and sacrifices had absorbed their stories, preserving them in its depths.

Enter the tale of the 'Zombie Miner'. Legend speaks of a miner, lost in a tragic accident deep within the tunnels. Some say it was a sudden tunnel collapse, others a devastating explosion, and still, others speak of the treacherous methane gases that claimed him. But death, it seems, was only the beginning of his journey. Trapped between the world of the living and the dead, he roams the forested expanse and the remnants of the mining pits, a ghostly figure with hollow eyes, appearing at dusk and disappearing by dawn.

To some, he's a spectral figure lost in time, seeking an exit from his eternal purgatory. To others, he's a cautionary tale, embodying the very essence of the dangers that the miners of yore faced. Yet, there's an undeniable sense of melancholy that surrounds him — a longing, perhaps, for the camaraderie he once knew, or maybe a desperate need to communicate a message from the afterlife.

In the subsequent chapters, you'll discover firsthand

accounts, tales passed down from generation to generation, and recent sightings that attest to the existence of this eerie entity. Whether myth, legend, or unsettling truth, the Zombie Miner of Cannock Chase beckons you into his world. Dare to delve deeper, and perhaps, just perhaps, you might catch a fleeting glimpse of those haunting eyes, watching, waiting, and forever bound to the echoes from the deep.

Mists of Brereton

Joan had always been an early riser. For as long as she could remember, she'd been one of those people who relished the quiet solitude that came with the dawn. It was in these twilight hours, as the world stirred from its slumber, that she'd take her trusty old Labrador, Max, for a walk. Their favourite spot was Brereton, especially the site of the old coal pits. There was a rugged beauty about the place, a silent testament to the industrial past of the area. But what Joan loved most was the peace and serenity that seemed to envelop the landscape, blanketed often by early morning mists.

On this particular morning, as the first light of day painted streaks of lavender and gold across the sky, Joan could feel an unusual chill in the air. She tightened her scarf around her neck and beckoned for Max to follow. Max, usually eager to explore, seemed oddly reluctant. Joan dismissed it as the old boy just showing his age, and they continued.

As they approached the old coal pits, the mist grew denser, curling around Joan's ankles and making the ground ahead less visible. The chirping of the morning birds seemed to fade, replaced by an eerie silence. Max started to growl low in his throat, his ears pinned back, eyes focused on something in the distance.

Joan followed his gaze but could only see the thick, white mist. "What's gotten into you, boy?" she whispered, trying to soothe him. But Max remained tense, his tail tucked between his legs, a clear sign of distress.

It was then that Joan heard it—a faint, rhythmic sound that echoed through the mist. It sounded like... tapping? No, it was more deliberate than that. It was the sound of a pickaxe meeting the earth. But that was impossible. The coal pits had been abandoned for decades. There was no mining activity here, not anymore.

As Joan strained her ears to locate the source of the sound, a figure began to emerge from the mists. It was a man, or what appeared to be a man, silhouetted against the dim light. His movements seemed laboured, his posture hunched. But what was most unnerving was the way he was dressed—in old, tattered mining gear, complete with a helmet and a glowing lantern by his side.

Frozen in place, Joan could only watch as the figure moved closer, his pickaxe swinging rhythmically by his side. Max whimpered, cowering behind her. As the miner came into clearer view, Joan felt her heart drop. His skin was an unnatural pallor, eyes hollow and void of life, and his lips were drawn back in an eternal grimace.

The realisation hit Joan like a ton of bricks. This was no ordinary man. This was the fabled Zombie Miner of Cannock Chase. Legends spoke of an undead miner who roamed the grounds, forever doomed to work the mines in the afterlife. Most locals dismissed it as mere folklore, tales spun to spook children or attract curious tourists. But here he was, right before Joan's very eyes.

He didn't seem to notice her, though. Instead, he moved with singular purpose, heading towards one of the old pit entrances, now overgrown with moss and ivy. As he reached the entrance, he paused, turning his hollow gaze towards Joan and Max.

For a heart-stopping moment, their eyes locked. Joan felt an overwhelming mix of sorrow and terror emanating from the apparition. It was as if he was trying to communicate, to share his eternal anguish. But before she could even react, the Zombie Miner turned away, disappearing into the pit, his lantern's glow slowly fading, leaving Joan in the enveloping mist.

It took Joan a few moments to snap out of her trance. Grabbing Max's collar, she made a hasty retreat, her heart pounding in her ears. She didn't stop until she reached her car, parked a good distance away.

Joan never went back to the Brereton coal pits. Instead, she'd share her encounter with anyone willing to listen, adding her tale to the many stories surrounding Cannock Chase. And while some sceptics would brush off her story as the byproduct of an overactive imagination, those who had felt the chilling mists of Brereton, those who had heard the faint echoes of a pickaxe, knew better.

For in the heart of England's strangest forest, the past is never truly gone. It lingers, waiting for the perfect moment to remind the living of the souls who once toiled beneath the earth, especially the one who is forever trapped in his undead state, eternally mining in the depths of despair.

Hednesford Hills' Haunting Hums

June 14, 1973, promised to be a splendid day for the Smith family. The sun had chosen to shine its brightest, the skies painted a flawless shade of blue, and there wasn't a hint of rain on the horizon. It was the perfect weather for a picnic. Margaret and John Smith, along with their children, Peter and Sarah, had picked Hednesford Hills as their ideal location.

The children's excited chatter filled the car as they approached their destination. Hednesford Hills, with its undulating landscapes and breathtaking views, had always been a favourite spot for the family. John had often regaled his children with tales of the hills' rich history, of battles and races, and of the miners who once toiled beneath the land.

Upon arrival, they found a serene spot atop one of the hills, offering a panoramic view of the surrounding countryside. The picnic basket was unpacked, and a spread was laid out on a blanket. Sandwiches, pies, fresh fruits, and lemonade, all contributed to the merry atmosphere.

As the afternoon sun cast long, dappled shadows, John strummed his guitar, and Margaret sang along, her melodious voice harmonising beautifully with the instrument. Peter and Sarah chased after one another, their laughter echoing in the vast openness.

However, as the sun began its descent, painting the sky with hues of orange and pink, the atmosphere changed. The first sign was a faint hum, distant and almost imperceptible. John, who had been tuning his guitar, paused. "Do you hear that?" he asked Margaret, who nodded slowly.

The hum grew more defined, transforming into a melody, a song that seemed oddly out of place. It sounded like a mining song, one of those melancholic tunes miners would sing to keep their spirits up as they delved into the bowels of the earth. But it wasn't just the song that was unsettling

—it was the fact that it seemed to be getting closer.

Sarah, who had been collecting wildflowers, clutched her bouquet and moved closer to her parents. Peter, always the more adventurous one, stood still, trying to discern the direction of the sound.

As the song grew louder, the lyrics became discernible: a lament about the perils of the mines, of darkness and danger, and of friends lost to accidents. The family sat, transfixed, as the melancholy tune wrapped around them.

And then, from the thickets on the other side of the hill, a shadowy figure emerged. It was a man, but not just any man. He wore old mining gear, tattered and covered in coal dust. A helmet sat atop his head, and in one hand he held a lantern that gave off an eerie, bluish glow.

The Zombie Miner of Cannock Chase.

The stories had been circulating for years, tales of an undead miner forever trapped in the throes of his past life. Most had dismissed these accounts as legends, stories spun around campfires to give people a thrill. But here he was, a spectre from the past, his hollow eyes fixed on the horizon as he sang his haunting tune.

Margaret, her maternal instincts kicking in, gathered her children close, her eyes never leaving the figure. John, although frozen in place, managed to whisper, "Stay calm, and don't make any sudden movements."

The Zombie Miner continued his song, moving slowly across the hill. His voice, though ethereal, carried the weight of years of toil and tragedy. The family could feel the coldness of the underground mines, the despair of being trapped, and the anguish of leaving loved ones behind.

As the last notes of his song faded, the figure stopped, turning his gaze towards the Smiths. A heavy silence fell upon the hill, broken only by the distant chirping of crickets. The Zombie Miner, his presence palpable, stared at the family for what seemed like an eternity. There was no malice in his eyes, only a profound sadness.

And then, just as suddenly as he had appeared, he turned

away, his lantern's glow illuminating his path as he disappeared into the thickets.

The Smiths remained still for several minutes, trying to process what they had just witnessed. John was the first to break the silence. "We need to leave," he whispered, his voice trembling.

They packed up their belongings in record time and made their way back to their car. The ride home was silent, each family member lost in their thoughts, the haunting melody of the mining song playing over and over in their minds.

The Smiths return to Hednesford Hills regularly, and their tale, like many others, adds to the growing legend of Cannock Chase and the Zombie Miner who roams its landscapes. The hills, with their deep-rooted history, have once again revealed a glimpse into a world where the past and present intertwine, reminding all who dare to venture there that some souls never truly find rest.

Littleton's Ghostly Locomotive

The year was 1996. Winter was setting in, and the skeletal branches of the trees surrounding Littleton bore testimony to the relentless cold that swept the land. The mining industry had undergone significant changes by this time, with many collieries facing closures. Littleton Colliery, once a bustling hub of activity, was now a silent testament to a bygone era.

Among the residents of the neighbouring village was an elderly gentleman by the name of Thomas Ridgeway. Born and raised in the shadow of the mines, Thomas had spent a large part of his youth working the tunnels beneath Cannock Chase. Though retired for many years, the stories of the mines and the legends that came with them remained fresh in his memory.

One evening, as the sun set and the village was wrapped in a soft, eerie mist, Thomas decided to take a walk, retracing the paths he'd so often tread in his younger days. He found himself drawn to the old Littleton Colliery rail tracks, now rusted and overgrown with weeds.

As he walked, the familiar sounds of the forest were all he could hear—the distant hoot of an owl, the rustling of leaves underfoot. But as the evening deepened, another sound began to reach his ears, one that had no place in the silent, abandoned setting.

It was the unmistakable chug of a locomotive engine.

Thomas stopped in his tracks, straining his ears to pinpoint the source. It couldn't be—a train hadn't passed these tracks in years. Yet, there it was, the rhythmic, persistent sound of an engine, the whistles echoing in the distance as if calling out to the souls of miners long gone.

And as Thomas stood there, a figure began to materialise from the mist, standing by the side of the tracks. The form was unmistakably that of a miner, complete with a tattered uniform and a helmet, its lamp emitting a feeble blue glow.

The face, though shadowed, bore the tell-tale signs of one who had spent years in the darkness of the mines—the hollow cheeks, the sunken eyes, the ashen skin.

The Zombie Miner.

The miner stood there, his gaze fixed on the tracks, as if waiting for a train that Thomas knew would never come. Every so often, he'd lift his lamp, its light cutting through the mist, looking up and down the tracks with an expression of hope mixed with eternal despair.

Thomas, rooted to the spot, felt a mixture of fear and sympathy. The stories he'd heard in his youth had never prepared him for an actual encounter. He considered calling out to the apparition but thought better of it. Instead, he stood silently, watching as the miner continued his endless vigil.

The distant sounds of the ghostly locomotive grew louder, the chugging and whistling echoing off the trees, enveloping the area in an otherworldly aura. And as the noise reached its crescendo, the miner's form began to waver, becoming more and more transparent until he vanished, leaving behind only the chilling sounds of the train.

Thomas, his heart racing, remained still for a few minutes, trying to comprehend what he had just witnessed. He had no doubt in his mind that he had come face to face with the legendary Zombie Miner of Cannock Chase.

Wordlessly, he turned and made his way back to the village. That night, he confided in his granddaughter, Emily, recounting the eerie events. Emily, always fascinated by the tales her grandfather would spin, listened with rapt attention. By morning, the story had spread throughout the village.

While some dismissed it as the ramblings of an old man, others weren't so sceptical, especially those who had experienced their own inexplicable encounters around Cannock Chase. They believed that the Zombie Miner's spirit was tethered to these lands, that he continued to relive his past, always waiting for a train to take him home, to reunite him with his loved ones, and to free him from his restless wandering.

Years later, when Thomas Ridgeway passed away, the villagers recalled his encounter, adding it to the growing collection of tales surrounding the Zombie Miner. But for Emily, it became a cherished memory of her grandfather—a reminder of the deep ties between the people, the land, and the legends that continue to shape Cannock Chase.

And to this day, on certain misty evenings, if one ventures near the old Littleton Colliery rail tracks and listens closely, they might just hear the distant sounds of a ghostly locomotive and catch a fleeting glimpse of a miner, forever waiting for a journey that will never begin.

Cannock Wood's Phantom Footsteps

It was August 2016. Summer had washed over Cannock Chase, painting it with a palette of vivid greens and the golds of sunlit afternoons. For the families and adventurers of the region, the sprawling heathlands, dense woodlands, and historical sites offered a respite from the routines of daily life. But while most were drawn to the obvious beauty spots of the Chase, some intrepid souls ventured towards the lesser-known mysteries, often inadvertently stumbling upon the region's darker tales.

Sarah and Mark Jones, a young couple with a shared passion for hiking, we're no strangers to the trails of Cannock Chase. The pair had mapped most of its territories, embarking on weekend excursions that ranged from the idyllic to the challenging.

But on this particular day, a recommendation from a fellow hiker had led them to the outskirts of Cannock Wood, the site where the famous mines once stood.

Though the mines had long since been closed and their entrances sealed, they had left behind an indelible mark on the landscape—telltale signs of earthworks, bits of industrial debris, and sunken areas that hinted at the labyrinthine tunnels below.

As the couple made their way deeper into the woods, Sarah couldn't shake off a strange feeling. There was an uncanny silence, broken only by the sound of their footsteps on the earthen trail. The forest, though beautiful in its overgrown wildness, cast long, undulating shadows that played tricks on the eyes.

About an hour into their hike, Mark paused to adjust the straps of his backpack. It was then that they both noticed it—the faint but unmistakable sound of footsteps echoing theirs. The steps seemed distant yet eerily close, a shadow dance of sound that defied their attempts to locate its source.

"Probably just another hiker," Mark suggested, trying to brush it off. But as they resumed their journey, the footsteps continued, growing louder, more insistent.

Sarah and Mark exchanged uneasy glances. Every time they stopped to listen, the footsteps halted. Every turn they took was mirrored by this unseen follower. "

As the afternoon wore on, the footsteps seemed to draw closer. At one point, Sarah thought she saw a faint imprint appear on the path behind them—a boot mark, aged and worn. They found another, and then another. A trail of footprints, materialising out of nowhere, yet no figure in sight.

Panicking, the couple decided to abandon their original path and make their way back to the main trail. The footsteps grew more frantic, echoing their hurried pace, as if chasing them. Their hearts raced, each thud resonating with the phantom steps that hounded them.

Finally, as they neared the edge of Cannock Wood, the footsteps ceased, and the oppressive atmosphere lifted.

Gasping for breath, Sarah and Mark took a moment to gather themselves. The forest, which had seemed so ominous just moments before, now bathed in the soft glow of the setting sun, appeared almost serene.

Upon returning to their car, the pair shared their experience with a local who was walking his dog nearby. The man, a weathered old soul with deep-set eyes, listened intently, nodding occasionally.

"It's not the first time I've heard such tales," he said, his voice raspy with age. "The Zombie Miner, they call him. He's been wandering these woods for decades, ever since the mines shut down. Some say he's looking for his fellow miners, lost to time. Others believe he's trapped in a liminal space, unable to find peace."

The man then shared his own encounter from years ago, a chillingly similar experience of being followed by unseen footsteps during a walk in the woods. Many, he explained, had such stories, though few spoke of them, fearing ridicule or disbelief.

Sarah and Mark left Cannock Wood that day with a story they would never forget, a brush with the supernatural that would forever colour their memories of Cannock Chase. For years, they would recount their encounter to friends and fellow hikers, often met with a mix of scepticism and genuine curiosity.

As the years go by and the incident becomes a distant memory, Cannock Wood continues to be a place of intrigue for many. And every so often, whispers emerge of hikers hearing phantom footsteps, of footprints appearing on forest trails, always hinting at the presence of the elusive Zombie Miner of Cannock Chase.

Though the veracity of these tales remains in the realm of the unknown, one thing is certain—for those who venture into Cannock Wood, the echoes of the past, both real and imagined, are ever-present, waiting to be discovered, waiting to be told.

The Shadows of Hawkins' Workshop

November 13th, 1999.

Fascination with the paranormal had been rapidly gaining momentum in the latter part of the 20th century. The era saw a surge in the desire to understand the unknown, to probe the mysteries that lay on the fringes of science and belief. For Martin Greaves, a self-proclaimed paranormal enthusiast, this curiosity was not just a hobby, but a deep-seated passion. His numerous explorations had led him to the haunted castles of Scotland, the ghostly pubs of London, and the eerie backroads of the English countryside.

However, one story had always eluded him: the legend of the Zombie Miner of Cannock Chase. The tale had been whispered in the darkened corners of pubs and among hikers who'd encountered the unexplainable in the dense woods. And many of the stories, many of the accounts, had one connecting thread – Hawkins' Workshop.

Once the heart of Cannock's mining tool production, Hawkins' Workshop was now but a skeletal reminder of its former glory. Abandoned for many years, the old brick and timber structure had gradually surrendered to the elements. Its windows were shattered, its roof collapsed in places, and nature had started to reclaim the walls and floor. But for Martin, this dilapidated building was the epicentre of paranormal activity.

With camera, tape recorder, and a journal in hand, Martin made his way to the workshop late one autumn afternoon. The sun was low, casting long shadows that danced and flickered with the breeze. The air was filled with the earthy scent of fallen leaves. All seemed normal, at first.

But as he stepped inside the crumbling structure, a palpable shift in the atmosphere took hold. It was as though the air itself was charged, waiting to release a century's worth of memories.

The first thing Martin noticed was the remnants of mining tools scattered about. Rusty pickaxes, hammers, and other implements lay strewn across the rotting workbenches and floor. He set up his equipment, keen on capturing any anomalies. And as the minutes passed, and the light outside began to wane, things took a turn for the bizarre.

One by one, the tools seemed to move of their own accord. A pickaxe handle tilted slightly. A hammer slid an inch across the table. It was subtle, but unmistakable. Martin felt a mix of excitement and trepidation. Was this the work of the fabled Zombie Miner?

With the descending darkness, Martin switched on his torch, its beam cutting through the gloom, revealing pockets of the workshop that had remained undisturbed for decades. And then, as he shone the light towards a particularly rusty sheet of metal propped against a wall, he saw it. A reflection. Not his own, but that of a gaunt, hollow-eyed figure, clad in the tattered remnants of a miner's uniform.

For a moment, time stood still. Martin's heart raced, his

breath caught in his throat. He slowly moved the flashlight away, then back again. The reflection remained, staring back at him with an inscrutable gaze. The room grew colder, the shadows deeper.

Gathering his courage, Martin tried to communicate. "Who are you?" he whispered, voice trembling.

There was no response, but the reflection shifted, its mouth opening slightly as if trying to form words, to convey a message lost to time.

The next few minutes were a blur. Martin snapped photos, his camera's flash illuminating the workshop in stark bursts of white light. With every flash, the reflection seemed to grow more tangible, more real. And then, as suddenly as it had appeared, it vanished.

Shaken, Martin quickly gathered his equipment and made his way out of the workshop. The forest outside seemed louder, more alive, as if it had been holding its breath, waiting for him to leave.

Back in the safety of his car, Martin reviewed his photos. Among the many shots of the decrepit workshop, one stood out. It was of the rusty metal sheet, and there, faint but visible, was a reflection he deemed to be that of the Zombie Miner.

The experience at Hawkins' Workshop solidified Martin's belief in the paranormal. He would go on to share his encounter with numerous paranormal communities and enthusiasts, adding his story to the growing lore of Cannock Chase.

But for Martin, the event held deeper significance. It was a testament to the lingering spirits of the past, of souls trapped in a limbo, seeking acknowledgment, seeking release. And every time he would retell his encounter, he'd end with a word of caution to fellow seekers of the unknown: "Respect the spirits, for they too were once living, with stories, dreams, and desires. And in the quiet corners of places forgotten by time, they still linger, waiting to be heard."

As for Hawkins' Workshop, it's long gone, but it was once a

silent witness to the passage of time. And those who ventured close, especially as the sun dipped below the horizon, would often report a feeling of being watched, of hearing faint whispers, and sometimes, if they were particularly observant, of catching a fleeting glimpse of a reflection that wasn't their own.

Rugeley's Resonating Remnants

September 12th, 2005

The sun was setting, casting a golden hue over the remnants of Rugeley's mining infrastructure. Once a bustling hub of coal extraction and now a melancholic relic of the past, the mining shafts had become a popular site for urban explorers and history enthusiasts. For Tom and Eleanor, a young couple with a penchant for adventure, it promised a day filled with intrigue.

Tom, a local to Rugeley, had grown up listening to tales of the mines and had even had a great-grandfather who worked there. Eleanor, on the other hand, was a city girl, eager to dive into the mysteries of the countryside. Tom wanted to show her the eeriness of the old tunnels and share some of the ghost stories he'd heard over the years, thinking it would be a fun and spooky experience for them both.

Their torches pierced the impending darkness as they approached the entrance of one of the oldest tunnels. The entrance, mostly covered with ivy and moss, exuded an old-world charm.
"Ready to embark on this historical adventure?" Tom asked, his voice betraying a hint of mischief.

Eleanor nodded, squeezing his hand tightly, her heart racing with a mix of excitement and anxiety. "Always up for a good scare," she responded with a grin.

As they ventured deeper into the mine, the echoes of their footsteps seemed to bounce back with an eerie resonance. Eleanor, ever the inquisitive one, began humming a tune to hear how it would reverberate in the shafts. The results were hauntingly beautiful, each note lingering in the air longer than it should.

Intrigued by this acoustical marvel, Tom began whispering

random phrases to see how they echoed. "Eleanor, will you marry me?" he whispered playfully, earning him a chuckle and a playful shove from his girlfriend.

However, to their surprise, a faint response echoed back, "Below... waiting...". The couple exchanged puzzled glances. Assuming it was an auditory illusion caused by the peculiar structure of the mine, they continued deeper.

Eleanor, growing more anxious with every step, finally voiced her unease. "Tom, do you ever get the feeling that we're not alone down here?"

Brushing off her worries, Tom reassured her, "It's just the echo, love. Old mines can play tricks on your senses. Besides, no one else knows about this particular entrance."

However, as the hours passed, even Tom couldn't ignore the subtle signs that something was amiss. There were cold spots, which were unusual given the otherwise consistent temperature in the mine. Whispers seemed to emanate from nowhere and everywhere at once, often incoherent, but occasionally forming words like "leave" or "danger".

Feeling increasingly uneasy, Eleanor suggested they make their way out. They had seen enough, and the chilling ambiance was wearing on her nerves. Tom agreed, although he tried to maintain a brave face, insisting that it was all in their heads.

But as they made their way back, a dim light began to flicker from one of the offshoot tunnels. It was an old-fashioned miner's lamp, its light dancing and illuminating the figure of a man. The figure looked worn and battered, with dirt-covered clothes that resembled the old uniforms of miners from a bygone era. Most disturbingly, his eyes were hollow, devoid of life, and yet they seemed to be staring straight at Tom and Eleanor.

Frozen in place, Eleanor squeezed Tom's hand, her eyes wide with terror. "Who... what is that?" she whispered.

Before Tom could answer, the figure began to advance towards them, his movements awkward and disjointed. As he neared, the whispers grew louder, forming a chorus of ghostly voices warning the couple to leave.

Eleanor, paralyzed with fear, could barely find her voice. "Run," she managed to utter, pulling Tom with her as they made a dash for the entrance.

The whispers grew louder and more desperate, echoing in their ears as they raced through the tunnel. Every so often, they would glimpse the flicker of the old-fashioned lamp, confirming that the figure was still in pursuit.

Finally, gasping for breath, the couple emerged from the mine, the entrance now bathed in the early rays of dawn. They didn't stop running until they reached Tom's car, parked a distance away.

As they drove off, Eleanor turned to Tom, tears streaming down her face. "What was that? What did we just see?"

Tom, equally shaken, could only respond, "I don't know, Ellie. I don't know."

Word of their encounter spread through Rugeley like wildfire. Many dismissed it as a prank or a figment of the couple's imagination. Yet, there were some older residents who whispered about similar encounters from decades past, about a miner who never made it out and still roamed the tunnels in search of salvation.

While Tom and Eleanor never returned to the mine, their experience became a testament to the mysterious events surrounding Rugeley's mining infrastructure. It was a reminder that some places, steeped in history and tragedy, never truly let go of their past.

And so, as visitors continue to explore the remnants of Rugeley's mines, they do so with a mix of curiosity and trepidation, always listening for the haunting echoes and watching for the dim light of the Zombie Miner.

Castle Ring's Cryptic Chronicle

Dr. Katherine Miles had always been enchanted by history. A distinguished archaeologist with several published papers to her name, Katherine had travelled extensively, unearthing relics that spoke of times long gone. Castle Ring, an ancient hill fort located in Cannock Chase, was her latest muse.

The site held strategic importance during the Iron Age and was teeming with remnants of its storied past. It was said to offer a panoramic view of the surrounding areas, allowing its ancient inhabitants to monitor any approaching threats. But what intrigued Katherine the most was the scattering of old mining artefacts that seemed to pepper the area around the hill. These artefacts were seemingly out of place amidst the fort's ruins.

Diligently, Katherine had spent days mapping out the area, noting the locations of these mining relics. They seemed to lead towards the forest's depth, hinting at the presence of long-forgotten mining tunnels beneath the trees.

One evening, engrossed in her work, Katherine lost track of time. The sun dipped below the horizon, shrouding Castle Ring in an ethereal twilight. As darkness slowly crept in, Katherine decided to call it a day. However, as she was packing up her equipment, something caught her eye.

An old miner's helmet lay half-buried in the soil, its metal rusted but the shape unmistakable. Curiosity piqued, Katherine brushed away the dirt, revealing a faded insignia. It looked like a family crest, but not one she recognized.

Holding the helmet, she felt an uncanny chill. The summer evening was still, yet the air around her grew cold, and the trees whispered as though carrying secrets of ages past. Katherine's practical mind chided her for letting the atmosphere get to her, but deep down, she couldn't shake off the feeling of being watched.

As she turned to leave, a movement at the periphery of her vision stopped her in her tracks. In the distance, a shadowy figure stood. It was the silhouette of a man, dressed in what appeared to be mining attire from the 19th century. His face was obscured by the dark, but his posture was that of deep contemplation.

Katherine blinked, attempting to clear her vision. But when she opened her eyes, the figure was unmistakably closer, still standing silent and motionless. Panic welled up inside her, but the archaeologist in her sought answers. She mustered up the courage to call out, "Who are you?"

The figure didn't respond verbally but slowly raised an arm, pointing towards the helmet in Katherine's hand.

Gathering her wits, Katherine responded, "This belongs to you?" She held up the helmet, hoping for some form of acknowledgment.

The figure took another step closer, the dim light revealing hollow eyes that held an abyss of sorrow. Those eyes, though empty of life, conveyed an emotion that tugged at

Katherine's heart: loss.

Suddenly, a rush of memories not her own flooded Katherine's mind. Visions of a mining accident, a cave collapsing, trapping miners, a desperate attempt to save a fellow miner—brother, perhaps—all ending in darkness. The raw emotion of the memory—pain, fear, regret—overwhelmed her.

Shaken, Katherine dropped the helmet, the impact breaking the connection and ending the flood of memories. The figure, now identifiable as the Zombie Miner, looked down at the helmet and then back at her, a silent plea in his haunting gaze.

As if understanding, Katherine whispered, "You want to be remembered, don't you?"

The figure nodded slowly.

Taking a deep breath, Katherine promised, "I'll ensure your story is told. You and the others won't be forgotten."

A soft wind rustled the trees, and when it passed, the figure was gone, leaving Katherine alone with the ancient relics and the promise she had made.

The following day, Katherine returned to Castle Ring, this time with a team. The findings over the next few weeks were unprecedented. Multiple mining artefacts were unearthed, painting a clearer picture of the mining activities that took place in Cannock Chase during the 1800s.

Among the discoveries was a journal, preserved against time's ravages, which gave a firsthand account of a tragic mining accident. It spoke of a brave miner who tried to save his colleagues, only to be trapped himself.

The journal and subsequent discoveries have never been released to the public. Katherine went on to document her findings and the strange encounter she had, but was prevented from publishing by her employer.

Word reached me in 2020, and I took a keen interest in Katherine's story. I interviewed her, hoping to shed more light on the mysterious figure of the Zombie Miner. I recorded Katherine's account meticulously, adding another chapter to the growing legend of the Zombie Miner of Cannock Chase.

Though Katherine had set out to uncover Castle Ring's secrets, she never anticipated crossing paths with a spectral miner, forever wandering in search of recognition. Her encounter that fateful evening not only rewrote history but also underscored the timeless adage: The past, though buried, is never truly forgotten.

Hednesford's Bewitching Breeze

The annual summer festival in Hednesford was an event locals and tourists alike looked forward to. The festival celebrated the region's rich history, combining it with modern merriment. Live music, delicious food stalls, historical reenactments, and games for children ensured the festival was packed with visitors of all ages.

Amidst the joy and laughter, a group of friends—Sophie, Jake, and Tessa—were enjoying the festivities. They had grown up together in Hednesford and had attended the festival every year since it began. This year was particularly special, as Jake was returning home after several years of studying abroad.

"I can't believe how much has changed, yet everything feels

the same," Jake remarked, biting into a locally made pork pie.

Tessa laughed, "That's the charm of Hednesford for you. New stalls and faces each year, but the heart of the place remains unchanged."

As the day waned, a local folk band took the stage, filling the air with nostalgic melodies. People clapped, danced, and sang along, completely immersed in the moment.

Sophie, ever the romantic, dragged Jake and Tessa away from the park and towards a quieter spot to watch the sunset. They found a small clearing near the entrance of one of the old Hednesford Mines. The sealed entrance served as a backdrop for photos during the festival, with fairy lights hung around it, creating an enchanting ambiance.

The three friends sat down, reminiscing about their childhood adventures. However, as the sun dipped below the horizon and the first stars appeared, an unusual cold breeze enveloped the area.

Jake shivered. "That's odd. It was so warm just a moment ago."

Tessa, wrapping her shawl tighter, agreed. "It feels like it's coming from the mines. But that's impossible, right?"

Sophie, her eyes squinting at the mine entrance, whispered, "Guys, do you see that?"

Emerging from the shadows near the mine entrance was the figure of a man, dressed in old-fashioned mining gear, covered in dust and grime. His face, pale and gaunt, appeared etched with fatigue and sorrow. The fairy lights, though dim, illuminated his hollow eyes, which seemed to be filled with a mixture of sadness and longing.

The trio, frozen in place, watched as the figure slowly made its way down the road and towards Hednesford Park. They weren't the only ones to notice. As the miner walked, a hush fell over other people in the vicinity too.

Jake, gathering courage, approached the figure, trying to understand if it was a prank or part of the festival's attractions. "Excuse me, are you part of the reenactment?"

The figure, without uttering a word, turned its gaze towards Jake, revealing a more detailed visage of wear and age. Jake felt a sudden rush of emotions—sadness, desperation, and a profound sense of loss.

Behind him, Tessa whispered to Sophie, "I've never seen or heard about this in any of our previous festivals. Who is he?"

Sophie, equally perplexed, replied, "I have no idea, but there's something hauntingly familiar about him."

Without warning, the miner turned and started walking back towards the mines. As he approached the sealed entrance, he paused, placing a hand on it, as if communicating with the spirits trapped within. After a long moment, he disappeared into the shadows from whence he came.

The cold breeze that had accompanied his appearance ceased, and warmth returned to the whole area. However, the atmosphere had irrevocably changed. The lively music and dancing was still present, but there were also hushed conversations and shared experiences amongst the locals who bore witness to the sighting. Some people spoke of the emotions they felt upon seeing the miner—feelings of sorrow, regret, and an unyielding desire for closure.

The trio, still processing their encounter, decided to seek answers. They approached one of the elder members of the Hednesford community, Mrs. Wilkins, known for her extensive knowledge of the town's history.

Mrs. Wilkins listened intently to their account and nodded slowly, "What you've witnessed is rare but not unheard of. Legends speak of miners who were trapped in accidents and never found their way out. Their spirits, restless and yearning for recognition, occasionally manifest, especially when the living celebrate near their resting places."

Sophie, her voice shaking, asked, "So, it wasn't a hoax or part of the festival?"

Mrs. Wilkins shook her head, "No, dear. What you

witnessed was a soul seeking acknowledgment."

While the festival resumed its jovial nature in subsequent years, for that particular year at least, the whole thing felt rather strange for quite a few people.

And so, as the tales of the Zombie Miner of Cannock Chase grew, the bewitching breeze of Hednesford's summer festival became a testament to the thin veil separating the past from the present and the living from the dead.

Wyrley's Weeping Willow

The forest of Cannock Chase has always held its secrets close to its heart, revealing them only to those daring enough to tread its paths after sundown. It was here, near the remnants of the long-abandoned Wyrley mine, that an anomaly of nature drew the attention of Megan and Lewis, two diligent students of environmental science. A willow tree of extraordinary size and vitality stood as an enigma, its sweeping branches casting shadows that seemed to dance with secrets of their own.

Unlike other trees that dotted the area, this particular willow displayed an uncanny robustness, its leaves a shade greener, its trunk thicker and more twisted, as though it bore the weight of countless tales. Local whispers spoke of the 'tree that hid a chilling secret,' but it was these very whispers that kindled the flame of curiosity in the young researchers. Armed with their scientific equipment and an unquenchable thirst for knowledge, they decided to camp out beside this mysterious willow, aiming to document its unparalleled growth and perhaps uncover the secret behind its vigour.

As the sun bid adieu and the veil of night slowly blanketed the forest, the duo started their observations. Their equipment beeped and hummed, recording atmospheric changes, soil composition, and moisture levels. The nocturnal creatures of Cannock Chase began their nightly serenades, setting the background score for what was supposed to be a regular night of field research.

However, as the clock's hands inched towards midnight, an eerie silence started to replace the forest's natural sounds. Megan felt the hair on the back of her neck stand up, an instinctual reaction to the thick, cloying fog that began to envelop their campsite. The cold mist seemed to rise from the very ground they stood upon, rapidly obscuring their view and drenching everything in a wet greyness.

Emerging from this fog was a sight neither of them was prepared for—a miner, but this was no ordinary man. His skin, as pale as the moonlight, clung to his bones. His eyes, devoid of life, were sunken pits that reflected no light, and his movements seemed like an eternal struggle against the chains of death that sought to pull him under. The very aura around this figure was one of decay and endless sorrow. Megan and Lewis were face-to-face with the legendary Zombie Miner, a spectral figure tied to countless tales of horror.

Frozen in their spots, the duo watched as the miner ambled closer to the willow. His soft moans, filled with anguish, echoed in the stillness. With every step he took, the ground seemed to pulsate in response, as though the very earth recognized the pain of this tormented soul. His skeletal fingers, decayed by time and tragedy, traced patterns over the willow's bark. Black, viscous tears streamed from his eyes, dripping onto the roots, which seemed to drink in this dark essence with a thirst that was almost palpable.

It dawned on Megan and Lewis that they were witnessing a communion of sorts. The tree, in its silent wisdom, seemed to be a beacon for this lost soul, a place of solace where his tormented spirit could find momentary reprieve. The hours that followed felt like an eternity. Time seemed to stretch, and the only constants were the Zombie Miner's mournful cries and the willow's silent acceptance of his grief.

With the first light of dawn, the thick fog began its retreat, and with it, the haunting figure of the miner. Drawn back into the shadows from whence he came, his silhouette faded, leaving behind a forest that seemed to breathe a sigh of relief.

As the sun climbed higher, Megan and Lewis tried to process the events of the night. Their initial intent of studying the tree had led them down a path of ancient tragedies and spectral encounters. Delving into the history of the Wyrley mine, they uncovered tales of mine collapses, trapped souls, and grieving families left behind. The pieces of the puzzle started to fit together. The miner's unresolved pain and the willow's inexplicable growth seemed intertwined, with the tree drawing its vitality from the very essence of the miner's anguish.

Though they had enough data for their research, the duo knew that some stories were too profound, too personal, to be shared. Choosing to keep their nocturnal observations between themselves, they left Cannock Chase with a newfound respect for the mysteries that nature, in collaboration with the past, could weave.

The Wyrley willow, forever intertwined with the legend of the Zombie Miner, remains a sentinel in the heart of the forest, a testament to the timeless dance between nature's wonders and the echoes of souls long gone.

Rawnsley's Radiant Lantern

November 2nd, 2007

Nestled on the outskirts of Cannock Chase, Rawnsley was a picturesque village that bore the timeless charm of historic England. Old streets echoed with the footsteps of those who had walked them for centuries, and every brick, every corner had a tale to tell. Yet, in this mosaic of stories, one particular legend overshadowed others. This was the tale of the radiant lantern, a mysterious beacon of hope that appeared in the darkest hours, casting light where there seemed to be none.

David Thompson was an avid traveller, a man accustomed to treading unfamiliar terrains and delving deep into local folklore. He had journeyed far and wide across the British Isles, collecting tales and anecdotes, often recounting them over campfires or in cosy taverns. Yet, even in his vast repertoire of stories, Cannock Chase stood out for its singularly haunting tales, especially that of the Zombie Miner. Sightings of this spectral figure had been reported from all corners of the forest, and while David had heard the tales, he had never experienced it himself.

On that fateful November evening, as David made his way to Rawnsley, he was met with an unexpected adversary. A thick blanket of fog had descended upon Cannock Chase, transforming its familiar landscape into an enigmatic maze. The path, which had been clear just hours ago, was now shrouded in mystery. With every turn he took, the surroundings became more unfamiliar, and an unsettling feeling of being lost began to creep upon him.

It was then, amidst the overwhelming gloom, that a glimmer of golden light pierced the fog. The soft, radiant glow seemed to beckon him, offering a path through the misty abyss. Drawn towards it, David found himself following a lantern that seemed to float in the air, its light unwavering and inviting.

The source of this light was a sight David had only heard of in stories. A miner, his features worn and weary, held the lantern. His clothes were tattered, his skin pallid, and his gait, while slow, was determined. This was the legendary Zombie Miner of Cannock Chase, a figure whose stories David had always listened to with a mix of scepticism and fascination.

With the lantern illuminating the path, David felt an unspoken assurance. Despite the miner's ghastly appearance, there was an aura of protection around him. The lantern's light wasn't just a guide through the physical darkness; it was a beacon of hope amidst despair, a reminder that even in the bleakest moments, one isn't truly alone.

Hour after hour, David followed the guiding light, the Miner leading him through paths less trodden, across silent brooks, and under the canopy of ancient trees. Their journey was marked by an uncanny silence, punctuated only by the soft crunch of leaves underfoot and the distant hoot of an owl.

As the night deepened, David's thoughts wandered to the

tales he'd heard about the Zombie Miner. Stories spoke of a dedicated miner, tragically caught in a mine collapse many decades ago. His spirit, bound to Cannock Chase, sought to protect and guide those who lost their way. While each account differed in details, the essence remained the same - a guardian spirit, eternally watchful.

By the time the first hint of dawn painted the sky, the fog had begun to lift. The lantern's glow, which had been David's only source of light, began to wane. And as the sun's first rays touched the ground, the figure of the Zombie Miner started to fade, his task complete. David found himself on a familiar path, Rawnsley's church spire visible in the distance.

Gratitude welled up within him, not just for being guided to safety, but for the rare experience he'd been gifted. The legend of the Zombie Miner was no longer just a tale for David; it was a lived reality.

Over the next few days, as David shared his encounter with the villagers and other travellers, he realised he wasn't alone. Many had similar tales of being led to safety by the mysterious lantern. The Zombie Miner, with his radiant light, had become a symbol of hope and protection in Cannock Chase. Each story, while unique in its details, echoed the same sentiment—a guardian spirit, eternally watchful, ensuring that no harm befell those who wandered the enigmatic expanse of the forest.

Rawnsley, and indeed all of Cannock Chase, revelled in this shared heritage, a bond formed through collective experiences and tales passed down generations. And while the forest remained a place of myriad mysteries, one thing was certain: in its heart, there existed an undying spirit, a miner of old, who watched, waited, and guided those who needed him the most.

Beaudesert's Broken Ballad

April 13th, 2003

The vast expanses of Cannock Chase, with its labyrinth of trees and winding pathways, has always been a reservoir of tales, each more chilling than the last. Beaudesert, a quaint region nestled in its heart, bore a tale so haunting that it turned the bravest of souls cold.

Sarah, an independent sound engineer with an appetite for natural soundscapes, decided to visit Beaudesert one fateful evening. Always in pursuit of unique ambient sounds, she set her recording equipment up under the dense canopy. The early evening air was thick with the intoxicating aroma of wildflowers, and the melodic chirping of birds serenaded the surroundings.

As the sun began its descent, painting the sky with brilliant hues, Sarah started to pick up an anomaly in her recordings—a distant, almost inaudible hum, seemingly out of place in the serene environment. Intrigued, she adjusted her equipment, trying to capture the sound more clearly.

The hum gradually formed discernible notes, evolving into a sorrow-laden tune. The melody was unlike anything Sarah had heard before, a haunting ballad that seemed to echo the pain and despair of a bygone era. As the evening darkened into night, the ballad became more profound, filling the forest with an eerie resonance.

Transfixed by the ethereal sound, Sarah followed its source, her feet treading softly on the damp forest floor. The moon, now high in the sky, cast an otherworldly glow, guiding her deeper into the heart of the forest.

The ballad grew louder, its melancholy notes pulling at her heartstrings. And then, as she reached a small clearing, she saw him. Bathed in moonlight was the spectral figure of a miner, his attire ragged, his face covered in soot, eyes hollow and yet full of anguish. The Zombie Miner, a phantom from Cannock Chase's many tales, was no mere legend. He stood there, real as the trees that surrounded him, lost in the depths of his mournful song.

Sarah's heart raced, a mix of terror and fascination. The sight before her was bone-chilling: the miner's translucent figure, illuminated by the soft moonlight, his haunting ballad a testament to a tragic past. Every note that escaped his lips seemed to carry centuries of sorrow.

Too terrified to move, she watched as the miner's fingers danced over an old, battered harmonica, producing the sorrowful tune she had been chasing. As the ballad progressed, its narrative unfolded—a tale of love lost, of dreams crushed beneath the weight of the earth, of a life taken too soon in the dark, suffocating tunnels below.

Suddenly, the miner stopped, his hollow eyes fixing directly on Sarah, piercing the very depths of her soul. The weight of his gaze was oppressive, each second stretching into an eternity. The forest seemed to hold its breath, waiting for his next move.

Then, breaking the suffocating silence, the Zombie Miner

resumed his ballad. But this time, it was different. The melody, once full of pain, now carried a desperate plea, reaching out, asking to be heard, to be remembered. Sarah felt an overwhelming urge to reach out, to comfort this tormented soul, but her fear anchored her to the spot.

As the ballad reached its climax, a chilling wind swept through the clearing, causing Sarah's equipment to malfunction. The recording, the sole evidence of her terrifying encounter, was disrupted, replaced by an ear-piercing static. The gust seemed to carry away the miner's song, and with one final, mournful note, the Zombie Miner began to fade away, his figure dissipating into the misty night air.

Sarah stood there, shaken to her core, the echoes of the ballad still ringing in her ears. The forest, once a source of serenity, now felt overwhelmingly ominous. Gathering her equipment, she made her way out of the woods, the weight of the encounter pressing heavily on her heart.

By the time she reached her car, dawn was breaking, casting a soft light over Cannock Chase. Sarah, drained and traumatised, drove away, the haunting notes of the miner's ballad forever etched in her memory.

Years would pass, but the chilling encounter near Beaudesert remained Sarah's most haunting experience. The ballad, the very essence of the Zombie Miner's pain, had become an inescapable melody in her mind, a constant reminder of the tormented soul forever bound to the depths of Cannock Chase.

And so, the legend grew, nourished by Sarah's harrowing encounter. Those who ventured near Beaudesert at twilight would sometimes whisper of hearing a distant, sorrowful tune carried by the wind—a broken ballad, a testament to a spirit trapped in perpetual despair, forever seeking solace in the heart of England's strangest forest.

Chasetown's Chilling Charade

February 23rd, 2007

Chasetown, a hamlet wrapped in the embrace of Cannock Chase, carries with it an enduring legacy of miners, their trials and tribulations etched into its very soil. At the heart of this historic town stands the miner memorial, a stoic tribute to the brave souls who once delved deep beneath the earth, some never to emerge again.

It was in the quiet hours of dawn that Jenny, a photographer with a penchant for capturing the early morning serenity, found herself at the memorial. The soft morning light, she believed, would cast a golden glow on the structure, imbuing her photographs with an ethereal quality.

As she set up her camera and adjusted the focus, she took a

moment to reflect on the miners, their faces immortalised in stone. Their expressions spoke of hardships endured and sacrifices made, and Jenny felt an overwhelming sense of reverence.

But as the first rays of the sun began to illuminate the memorial, a thick, unnatural fog rolled in, blanketing the entire area. The sudden change in atmosphere sent a shiver down Jenny's spine. It wasn't the usual mist that sometimes accompanied the early morning hours. This was different—thicker, almost suffocating, and with an eerie stillness to it.

Struggling to see through the dense fog, Jenny noticed a vague silhouette emerging in the distance. As the figure drew nearer, its features became more distinct—a miner, his attire reminiscent of a bygone era, complete with a battered helmet and a dimly glowing lantern in his hand.

Jenny's heart raced. She had heard tales of the monsters of Cannock Chase but had always dismissed them as mere folklore. But now, the creature before her was impossible to ignore. The figure, seemingly unaware of her presence, slowly made his way to the memorial, his movements deliberate, yet heavy with sorrow.

The Zombie Miner knelt down before the stone faces of his comrades, placing his lantern beside him. He then proceeded to touch each name engraved on the memorial, pausing momentarily as if whispering a silent prayer or sharing a brief memory. His actions seemed to be a ritual of respect, a heartbreaking display of camaraderie even in death.

Frozen in place, Jenny watched, her camera forgotten. The very air around her seemed charged with emotion, and she could almost hear the faint echoes of a time long past—the distant rumble of the mines, the laughter and camaraderie of the miners, and the mournful tolling of bells signifying a life lost in the dark abyss below.

As the Zombie Miner continued his ritual, a chilling wind swept through the memorial, causing the lantern's flame to flicker wildly. The light it cast danced upon the stone faces, breathing life into them for a brief, haunting moment. The memorial, for those few seconds, was alive with the memories of the departed.

Suddenly, with an ear-piercing scream, the very earth seemed to tremble, echoing the calamities that had once befallen the miners. Jenny felt a rush of cold air, and the ghostly miner's head snapped up, his hollow eyes locking onto hers. Those eyes, devoid of life yet brimming with pain, bore into Jenny, making her very soul quiver with terror.

Without warning, the Zombie Miner let out a mournful cry, the sound echoing through the mist-laden air, sending a wave of dread throughout Chasetown. The cry was filled with the anguish of a tormented soul, forever bound to the land he had given his life to.

And then, just as suddenly as he had appeared, the terrifying figure began to fade away, his form descending into the thick fog. The lantern's glow dimmed until it was no more, leaving Jenny in darkness, her heart pounding loudly in the chilling silence.

Hours seemed to pass before the fog lifted and daylight broke through, returning the memorial to its peaceful state. Jenny, her body trembling and her mind struggling to comprehend the harrowing encounter, finally mustered the courage to leave, her camera and its untouched photos a testament to the morning's events.

The chilling charade she had witnessed would forever haunt Jenny. The ghostly miner's mournful tribute to his fallen comrades became an inescapable memory, a stark reminder of the sacrifices made by the brave souls of Chasetown.

As word of Jenny's encounter spread, many locals nodded in sombre agreement. While they had not seen the apparition themselves, they had felt its presence—a cold, unsettling breeze, a sudden fog, or the faint echo of a bygone era. They believed it was the Zombie Miner, returning time and again to honour his fallen friends, forever bound to the land that had both given and taken so much.

Norton Canes' Nostalgic Nocturne

June 14th, 2013

The sky was draped in a rich tapestry of deep blues and purples, the last remnants of the day surrendering to the impending reign of night. A silvery moon hung low, casting shimmering reflections upon the still waters beneath Norton Canes' old transport bridge. To many, the area was a testament to a time now lost—a relic of the past. But for Philip, a seasoned fisherman with a rugged beard and calloused hands, it was a sanctuary. Here, amidst the gentle sounds of water lapping at the banks and the soft croak of distant frogs, he found peace.

With his trusty fishing rod in hand, Philip settled into his usual spot, the worn-out wooden boards of the bridge offering familiar comfort. The water, illuminated by the moonlight, seemed ethereal—like a mirror into another world. Philip cast his line, watching as the lure disappeared into the depths with a soft plop. The quiet of the night enveloped him, and he leaned back, lost in thought.

As the hours meandered on, Philip's mind began to drift, the rhythmic dance of the water coaxing him into a near-trance. However, this serenity was soon interrupted by an odd sensation—a prickling feeling at the nape of his neck, as if he were being watched.

Drawing his focus back to his surroundings, Philip scanned the expanse of the bridge and its adjoining banks. That's when he saw it—a figure standing a distance away, its silhouette distorted by the moon's glow. The shape was unmistakably that of a miner, complete with a battered helmet and the shadowy outlines of a pickaxe. But it was the figure's eyes that sent a wave of cold dread coursing through Philip's veins. They glowed—a soft, eerie luminescence that seemed out of place, even in the pale moonlight.

The miner seemed engrossed in his own activity. In a motion mirroring Philip's own, he cast a line into the water, the gesture eerily silent. Yet, despite the quietude, the scene was charged with an unnatural tension, a heaviness that settled like a weight upon Philip's chest.

Dread rooted Philip to the spot. His initial inclination was to call out, but a primal fear held his voice hostage. The world around him seemed to blur, with only the figure of the miner remaining sharp, its every move a haunting dance in the moonlight.

Then, the wind began to change. What was once a gentle breeze now carried with it the unmistakable scent of damp earth and the distant, muffled sounds of a mine in operation —the clinking of tools, the muted conversations of miners, and, most chillingly, the occasional scream of despair.

The figure began to move, its steps deliberate and heavy, the sound echoing in the still night like the mournful tolling of a bell. With every step, the water around the bridge began to roil and churn, revealing glimpses of other ghostly faces beneath the surface, their hollow eyes fixed on Philip, their hands outstretched in a silent plea.

As the miner drew closer, Philip could see the details that confirmed his most terrifying suspicion: the pallid, rotting skin that clung to the miner's bones, the gaping wounds that hinted at a violent end, and the maw of a mouth, seemingly stuck in an eternal scream. This was no ordinary man; this was the Zombie Miner of Cannock Chase, a creature of legend, whose tales Philip had always dismissed as mere myths.

The chilling realisation hit him like a speeding train, and an instinctive urge to flee took over. But as he tried to move, the boards beneath him began to creak and groan, the very bridge itself seeming to come alive, its wooden planks contorting into anguished faces, trapping him in place.

The space between Philip and the zombie miner dwindled rapidly, the creature's haunting eyes never leaving Philip's own. And then, just as the distance had all but disappeared, the miner stopped. Slowly, it turned its gaze back to the water, lifting its line to reveal a catch—some kind of zombie fish, its form shimmering in the moonlight.

For what felt like an eternity, the world stood still. The only sound was the soft splash of the fish as the miner released it back into the depths. And then, without a backward glance, the zombie miner retreated into the shadows, the bridge returning to its inanimate form, and the chilling sounds of the underground fading away.

Philip, his heart still racing, quickly packed up his gear and fled, the horrifying events of the night etched into his memory.

In the days that followed, the trauma of that night weighed heavily on Philip. Sleep was elusive, and every shadow seemed to conceal the lurking figure of the Zombie Miner. The once-beloved bridge now represented a portal to a nightmare, one that Philip had no intention of revisiting.

However, as the weeks turned into months and the months into years, the raw terror of that night began to subside, replaced by an overwhelming need to understand. Why had the Zombie Miner appeared to him? Was it a mere chance encounter, or was there a deeper significance?

Yet, some questions are best left unanswered. The waters beneath Norton Canes' old transport bridge hold many secrets, and as Philip learned that fateful night, some are best left undisturbed.

Mill Green's Mournful Murmurs

The sun hung low over Mill Green, casting long, eerie shadows that danced and played as the wind rustled through the trees. The laughter of children echoed through the air, their innocence a stark contrast to the heavy weight of history that hung over the place. They ran freely, their small feet pounding against the ground, their worries limited to games of tag and hide-and-seek.

Among these children was eight-year-old Rosie, her golden locks bouncing as she dashed between trees, hiding from her friends. Giggling, she nestled behind a particularly large oak, pressing her body close to the bark, believing she'd found the perfect hiding spot.

As she waited, listening intently for the approaching

footsteps of her seekers, she felt the wind shift. A cold breeze caressed her face, making her shiver. As it passed, a hushed whisper reached her ears, chilling her to the bone.

"Stay safe..."

The voice was raspy, worn out by time, yet carrying an unmistakable note of concern. Startled, Rosie peeked from behind the tree, half-expecting to see one of her friends. But there was no one. Instead, a dense fog began to roll in, blanketing Mill Green in a shroud of mist.

Another whisper, closer this time. "Watch out..."

Rosie's heart pounded in her chest. She felt an undeniable presence, as if someone was nearby, watching over her. The once familiar nature reserve now seemed alien, its features distorted by the encroaching mist.

The laughter of her friends grew distant, drowned out by the soft murmurs that seemed to come from all around. Rosie felt trapped, the whispers drawing closer, the weight of unseen eyes pressing down on her.

Then, from the thick veil of the fog, a figure began to take shape. Tall and lanky, its silhouette was unmistakably that of a miner—complete with a hardhat and pickaxe. But it was the face that made Rosie's blood run cold. Pallid, rotting flesh clung to its bones, eyes sunken yet glowing with an eerie light.

Yet, as terrifying as the sight was, the Zombie Miner's demeanour wasn't threatening. Instead, he appeared almost sorrowful, his gaze sweeping over Mill Green as if searching for something—or someone. Every so often, he would pause, whispering words of caution to the wind, his voice laden with anguish.

Rosie, paralyzed by fear, watched as the figure slowly drifted towards a group of children playing near the pond—a place parents often warned their kids to stay away from due to its potential dangers. The whispers grew more frantic, the urgency in the miner's voice unmistakable.

"Stay back... Dangerous..."

The children, oblivious to the danger and the zombie

protector trying to warn them, continued their play. One of them, a little boy named Danny, edged dangerously close to the pond, peering curiously into its dark abyss.

The Zombie Miner's movements became frenzied. He lunged towards Danny, his outstretched hand mere inches from the boy. But instead of the expected cold touch of death, Danny felt a gust of wind pushing him backward, away from the crumbling edge.

As the boy stumbled, the fog began to dissipate, the figure of the Zombie Miner disappearing into the distance, his mournful murmurs echoing one last time across Mill Green.

Rosie, her breath coming in ragged gasps, made her way to Danny, relief flooding her as she realised he was unharmed. The other children, unaware of the spectral intervention, simply laughed off Danny's near fall, attributing it to his usual clumsiness.

But Rosie knew. She had witnessed the protective presence of the Zombie Miner—his eternal watch over Mill Green, ensuring no harm befell its innocent visitors.

That evening, as Rosie recounted the day's events to her grandmother, the old woman listened intently, her ace a mask of deep contemplation. Once the tale was done, she sighed, her voice barely above a whisper.

"Mill Green has always been protected, my dear," she began. "Years ago, a terrible accident in the mines claimed the lives of many men. They say one of them, a father who lost his life while trying to save others, was never able to move on. His love for children, especially his own, bound him to Cannock."

Rosie listened, her eyes wide, the weight of her encounter sinking in. The terrifying figure, with his decaying visage and glowing eyes, wasn't a creature of malice. He was a guardian, bound by tragedy, watching over the children of Mill Green.

Night fell, and as Rosie lay in bed, the haunting image of the Zombie Miner lingered in her mind. But instead of fear, she felt gratitude. For she knew that, beneath the moonlit canopy of Mill Green, a mournful spirit would always keep watch, ensuring the safety of all who played within its bounds.

Leacroft's Lamenting Lullaby

September 13th, 2011

Amidst the dense foliage and winding paths of Cannock Chase, one could often find solace in the untouched beauty of nature. But not every part of this verdant expanse was filled with peace. The area around Leacroft, particularly, was cloaked in an eerie silence, disturbed only by the occasional chirp of a bird or rustling of the leaves.

On this particular evening, the setting sun painted the sky with hues of orange and red, casting a soft glow that seemed to set the trees alight. Tucked away in a clearing, with an old, worn guitar in his hands, sat Ethan. The strings of the instrument bore the marks of years of passionate play, and Ethan, with his unkempt beard and piercing eyes, looked every bit the wandering musician he was.

With a deep breath, he began to strum, his fingers moving gracefully over the fretboard, conjuring a melancholic melody that seemed to resonate with the very soul of the forest. The tune he played was an old folk song, one he had learned during his travels, its origins unknown to him.

As the first few notes floated into the air, an unsettling chill permeated the surroundings. The gentle breeze that had been playfully tousling Ethan's hair suddenly turned cold and biting. And then, something truly uncanny occurred.

From the depths of the forest, a mournful hum began to rise, harmonising perfectly with the notes Ethan played. It was not the song of a bird or the howl of a distant animal, but a distinctly human voice, carrying with it a weight of endless sorrow.

Startled, Ethan ceased playing, the strings of his guitar producing a jarring discordant note. The haunting hum, too, stopped abruptly, replaced by an oppressive silence.

Feeling a mix of fear and intrigue, Ethan called out, "Who's there?" His voice seemed to echo endlessly, with no response forthcoming. He was about to dismiss the incident as a mere trick of the wind when he felt an unseen force tug at his guitar.

Without warning, the instrument came to life on its own, the strings vibrating as if played by ghostly fingers, producing the same melancholic tune. The mournful hum returned, this time louder, closer. It felt as though the forest itself was lamenting, mourning some long-lost love.

Out of the thickening mist, a figure slowly emerged. Tall and gaunt, with rotting flesh clinging to its skeletal frame, the creature bore the unmistakable appearance of a miner. Its eyes, though sunken deep into their sockets, glowed with a pale blue light, and it clutched a rusted pickaxe in its bony hand.

Horrified, Ethan tried to move, but his legs refused to obey, rooted to the spot by sheer terror. The Zombie Miner, as if compelled by the music, drew closer, the sorrow in its eyes palpable. It seemed to be searching for something, or perhaps someone, lost to the annals of time.

Suddenly, the guitar strings snapped, breaking the spell. The mournful hum ceased, and the Zombie Miner stopped in its tracks, its gaze now fixated on Ethan.

A heavy, oppressive atmosphere descended upon the clearing, and Ethan could feel the weight of centuries of sorrow bearing down on him. But rather than a sense of malice, the eyes of the Zombie Miner conveyed an endless despair, a longing for something forever out of reach.

Taking a deep, shuddering breath, Ethan slowly began to play once more, this time a soft, soothing lullaby, an attempt to ease the spirit's pain. The Zombie Miner seemed to respond, its posture less menacing, the glow in its eyes dimming slightly.

For what felt like hours, musician and spirit were locked in a duet of sorrow and comfort, the haunting beauty of their combined melodies echoing throughout the forest.

But as the last notes faded away, and Ethan's fingers stilled, the Zombie Miner let out a gut-wrenching scream of anguish. The force of it sent Ethan sprawling, and the world around him seemed to spin.

When he finally managed to regain his senses, the spectral figure was gone, leaving behind only the lingering echoes of its lament.

Shaken to his core, Ethan packed up his guitar and left the clearing, vowing never to return. But the haunting memory of that evening, the sorrow-filled eyes of the Zombie Miner, and the mournful melodies they had shared, would stay with him forever.

To this day, those who venture near Leacroft on quiet evenings claim to hear the faint strains of a lullaby, carried on the wind, a testament to the eternal bond formed between a wandering musician and a lost spirit, forever bound to the forest of Cannock Chase.

West Cannock No1 Colliery's Silent Pursuit

The remnants of West Cannock No1 Colliery, though long abandoned and reclaimed by nature, still would cast a daunting shadow over the landscape for many years after its closure. Overgrown foliage camouflaged the entrances to its dark tunnels, but locals knew better than to explore its depths. Despite the beauty of the surrounding Cannock Chase, this particular spot was avoided, becoming a dark legend amongst thrill-seekers and adventurous souls.

On this fateful evening, two such seekers of thrill, Mark and Claire, found themselves near the old colliery site. The duo were seasoned urban explorers and had heard whispers of the colliery's mysterious allure. The thrill of the unknown and the possibility of unearthing forgotten history was what drove them, and tonight was no different.

The late summer sun began its descent, painting the sky in fiery hues. Mark, with his camera in hand, began snapping pictures of the broken infrastructure. Claire, ever the careful one, took notes on their discoveries, her flashlight casting a narrow beam into the murky surroundings.

As the light dwindled, the pair decided to explore one of the partially concealed entrances to the underground labyrinth. With a sense of trepidation, they ventured in, the atmosphere growing denser with each step.

Deep within, away from the dying embers of the sunset, darkness was absolute. Their flashlights became their lifeline, creating islands of visibility in an ocean of pitch black. The musty scent of decay was thick in the air, mingling with a cold, metallic tang that made them uneasy.

As they progressed deeper, a growing sensation of being watched began to creep over Claire. Every shadow seemed to shift just beyond the edge of her flashlight's reach. The silence was oppressive, only broken by their own footsteps and the occasional drip of water from the ceiling.

Suddenly, Claire felt a cold gust of wind, unusual given the depth they were at. The beam of her flashlight caught something—a fleeting glimpse of a tall figure, gaunt, with tattered clothing that hinted at a miner's outfit. But it was its eyes that froze her in place—hollow sockets with an eerie glow that seemed to bore into her soul.

Panicking, Claire let out a scream, causing Mark to whirl around. But the figure had vanished as quickly as it appeared. Mark tried to calm Claire, suggesting it was just her imagination playing tricks on her. Yet, even he couldn't deny the electric charge in the air, a sensation of impending doom.

Deciding it was time to leave, they retraced their steps. But the once-familiar path now seemed distorted, as if the very walls were shifting. Every echo, every sound, magnified their rising panic.

Without warning, a heavy footfall sounded behind them. Mark and Claire turned their flashlights and saw the same ghastly figure, now unmistakably real and far too close. Its gaunt face bore the unmistakable signs of decay, while the rest of its body was a silhouette of terror. The Zombie Miner was no mere legend.

Mark grabbed Claire's hand, urging her to run. Their footsteps echoed in frenzied tandem as they tried to escape the relentless pursuit of the Zombie Miner. Twisting and turning through the dark passages, they felt him always just a breath away. His presence was overwhelming, a mix of malice and sorrow.

In their frantic escape, Claire tripped over some debris, her flashlight flying out of her hand and plunging them into darkness. Mark tried to pull her up, but before he could, cold, bony fingers wrapped around Claire's ankle, dragging her away.

Mark, in sheer desperation, grabbed a discarded iron rod, swinging it at their pursuer. The metal connected with a sickening thud, but the Zombie Miner seemed unfazed. Instead, with Claire in his grasp, he slowly turned his hollow gaze to Mark, a silent message in those depths.

Suddenly, Claire felt an unexpected sensation. Instead of

pain, there was a gentle warmth spreading from where the Zombie Miner touched her. The surroundings shifted, and visions began to play in her mind's eye: A time when the colliery was bustling, filled with miners, including the very being that held her. A tragic accident, a collapse, trapped souls... and among them, this miner, who just wanted to save others from the same fate.

As the visions faded, Claire found herself back in the tunnel, the Zombie Miner releasing her. The terror that had filled her moments ago was replaced by a deep sense of sadness. She realised that the chase, the pursuit, was not out of malevolence but a twisted form of protection, a desperate attempt to keep them away from the colliery's dangerous depths.

Mark, seeing Claire unharmed, helped her to her feet, and together, they made their way out, the weight of their encounter pressing heavily upon them.

Emerging into the night, the chilling experience at West Cannock No1 Colliery became a silent pact between them, a story too terrifying to share. But the legend of the Zombie

Miner, though terrifying, was not one of evil but of a lost soul, forever bound to the shadows of Cannock Chase, seeking to protect others from the dark fate he himself had suffered.

Shoal Hill's Silent Sentry

Shoal Hill, known for its sprawling grasslands and diverse birdlife, was a popular spot for birdwatchers. Amateur ornithologists would often set up camp with their binoculars, eager to catch a glimpse of the elusive species that graced the landscape. Among them was Daniel, an avid birdwatcher who'd been frequenting the hill for years.

One crisp autumn morning, as the fog clung to the ground and the sun threatened to pierce through, Daniel arrived earlier than most. He had always believed that the early hours, when the world was still quiet, were the best times to observe nature in its purest form.

Setting up his tripod, he scanned the horizon, the chirping of birds acting as a soothing background melody. As minutes turned into hours, Daniel became absorbed in his hobby, losing track of time.

It was during one of these moments of deep concentration, with his eye pressed against his binoculars, that he felt it—a sudden drop in temperature. Daniel pulled away, rubbing his arms for warmth. As he did, he noticed an old miner's helmet, tarnished with age, placed neatly next to his equipment.

Baffled, Daniel looked around, searching for anyone who might have placed it there. But he was alone, the vast expanse of Shoal Hill stretching out before him with no soul in sight.

Curiosity piqued, he picked up the helmet. It was heavy, its metal cold and oddly damp. Inside, he could make out faint initials, worn away by time, making them unreadable. As he held it, a faint whisper, almost like wind passing through trees, seemed to emanate from the helmet, sending chills down his spine.

Suddenly, a strong gust of wind swept across the hill, causing Daniel to lose his balance. Regaining his footing, he glanced around, and that's when he saw it. A few metres away stood a tall, gaunt figure dressed in old miner's attire.

Its skin was pallid, eyes hollow yet filled with an eerie light. The Zombie Miner, though Daniel didn't know it, stood silently, observing him just as he observed the birds.

Fear gripped Daniel, every fibre of his being urging him to flee. Yet, there was something oddly entrancing about the figure. It made no move to approach, merely watching, its attention occasionally diverted to the birds soaring above.

Moments felt like hours, the world around them fading as Daniel and the spectral miner continued their silent standoff. The wind carried with it whispers of old mining songs, tales of loss and longing, which only added to the overwhelming atmosphere of sorrow.

It was a raven's caw that broke the spell. The bird, large and inky black, landed on the helmet in Daniel's hand, regarding him with its keen eyes. As if on cue, the Zombie Miner shifted, his gaze fixated on the raven.

In an instant, the atmosphere changed. The sorrowful air was replaced with one of menace. The Zombie Miner's hollow eyes seemed to glow brighter, and a low, guttural growl, unmistakably inhuman, emanated from him.

Without a second thought, Daniel dropped the helmet, leaving his equipment behind as he sprinted away. The ground beneath him felt unstable, as if the very earth was trying to pull him under. Every rustle of grass, every chirp of the birds, seemed amplified, making his heart race even faster.

As he ran, he dared a glance back and was met with a sight he'd never forget. The Zombie Miner, with unnatural speed, was closing in, his figure elongating, becoming more grotesque with every step. The raven from before soared overhead, its caws echoing the miner's haunting pursuit.

Just as Daniel felt the cold grasp of the Zombie Miner inches from him, he tripped, tumbling into a concealed ditch. Moments passed, the silence absolute save for Daniel's ragged breathing. Cautiously, he peered out. The hill was empty, no sign of the terrifying entity that had chased him.

Climbing out, Daniel hastily gathered his equipment, the discarded miner's helmet now nowhere in sight. With one last look at the seemingly serene Shoal Hill, he made his way back to his car, the traumatic events playing on a loop in his mind.

The allure of Shoal Hill, once a haven for Daniel, had forever transformed into a landscape of terror. Though he never returned, the memory of that day remained etched in his mind, a haunting reminder of the time he crossed paths with the enigmatic and horrifying sentinel of Shoal Hill—the Zombie Miner.

Coppice Colliery's Cautious Caress

The abandoned site of Coppice Colliery had long intrigued locals and outsiders alike. Once a buzzing hub of activity, the mine had fallen into disuse and was reclaimed by nature. Vines and overgrowth concealed the entrance, and trees stood sentinel around its perimeter, guarding its dark secrets. The place carried an aura of times gone by, the silence punctuated only by the distant songs of birds and the occasional rustling of leaves.

On this particular day, a group of three adventurers, Matthew, Clara, and Neil, had decided to explore the site. They had heard tales of the mine's rich history but were unaware of the stories surrounding the Zombie Miner. With backpacks filled with essentials and torches in hand, they approached the foreboding entrance.

The trio's laughter and banter filled the air as they stepped into the mine's mouth. As they delved deeper, the sunlight became a faint glow, and the temperature dropped noticeably. Neil, ever the joker, made ghost noises, earning playful shoves from his companions.

It wasn't long before the atmosphere within the mine began to shift. The once clear path became a labyrinth of tunnels. Every echo, every distant drip of water seemed amplified, heightening the sense of isolation.

Matthew, leading the group, halted suddenly, causing Clara and Neil to bump into him. "Did you feel that?" he whispered. Before they could respond, a chilling gust of wind swept through the tunnel. It wasn't just the sudden drop in temperature that was unsettling; the wind seemed to carry with it hushed voices, murmuring tales of bygone mining days.

The three exchanged uneasy glances. "It's just the wind," Neil muttered, trying to convince himself as much as the others.

They proceeded with heightened caution, their torches revealing worn-out mining equipment and tools, frozen in time. The deeper they ventured, the more pronounced the whispers became. Faint sounds of pickaxes striking rock, the distant chatter of miners, and the soft hum of a lullaby wafted through the tunnels.

Suddenly, Clara's torch illuminated a figure at the end of a corridor. It was tall, its outline jagged and gaunt. Its eyes, though hollow, gleamed with an ethereal glow. The Zombie Miner stood there, its appearance both pitiful and terrifying.

Frozen in place, the trio could only stare. The miner raised a bony finger to his lips, motioning for silence, then beckoned them closer.

Against their better judgement, the three were drawn towards him. As they neared, the whispers grew louder, more distinct. They were tales of mining accidents, cave-ins, and lost souls, all culminating in the legend of the Zombie Miner—a once proud worker who met a tragic end but never left the colliery.

Reaching out, the Zombie Miner's skeletal hand caressed Clara's cheek. It was a gesture filled with sadness, longing, and a touch of menace. The coldness of his touch sent a jolt through her, breaking the trance.

Clara's scream echoed throughout the mine. The Zombie Miner, his gaze now filled with anguish, began to advance, the distance closing rapidly.

Panic took over, and the trio sprinted back the way they came, the haunting whispers now replaced by the miner's mournful cries. The once familiar tunnels seemed to twist and turn, their escape route now a confusing maze.

Just when they thought they had lost their pursuer, Neil was violently pulled back, his screams filling the air. Matthew and Clara turned to see their friend being dragged into the darkness by the relentless Zombie Miner.

Mustering all her courage, Clara hurled her torch at the advancing figure. The sudden brightness seemed to stall him, buying them precious seconds. Grabbing Matthew's hand, Clara pulled him forward, their desperate escape fueled by adrenaline.

After what felt like hours, the faint glow of the mine's entrance came into view. Bursting out into the sunlight, the two collapsed, gasping for breath, the horrors of the mine replaying in their minds.

Neil was never seen again. Matthew and Clara, forever scarred by the events, tried to share their story, but few believed them. The legend of the Zombie Miner, however, grew, with many avoiding Coppice Colliery, fearful of encountering the mournful spirit that still roamed its depths, whispering tales of mining days and watching over his eternal domain.

Gentleshaw's Guiding Glow

For Charlotte and Isaac, what started as an innocent day hike near Gentleshaw turned into a night they would never forget.

The couple had embarked on their journey early in the morning, their goal to explore the natural beauty of the area. They were no strangers to hiking, often spending weekends navigating various terrains. This particular day, they had chosen a new path, intrigued by its untamed allure.

However, as the day wore on and the sun began its descent, they realised they had veered off the intended path. Their surroundings began to look unfamiliar, and an eerie sense of unease settled over them. The thickening fog that began to roll in made visibility difficult, and every direction seemed indistinguishable from the next.

"It's okay," Isaac reassured Charlotte, even though his voice betrayed a hint of worry. "We just need to find a landmark or a path. It's easy to get turned around in these woods."

But as darkness truly began to take hold, so did their fear. The forest sounds seemed to magnify. Twigs snapping, the distant hoot of an owl, the rustling of leaves in the wind - all painted a soundscape that further disoriented them.

Charlotte clutched Isaac's arm. "Did you hear that?" she whispered. From somewhere deep in the forest, they heard a faint humming - a melancholic tune that seemed both comforting and unnerving.

And then, in the distance, a dim light began to pierce through the fog. It was subtle at first but gradually grew stronger, a gentle glow moving steadily closer.

"It must be another hiker," Isaac mused, relief evident in his voice. "Hey! Over here!" he called out, waving his arms.

But as the light drew nearer, Charlotte felt a pit forming in her stomach. The glow was emanating from an old lantern, held aloft by a figure that was anything but human. Its form was decayed, skin pallid and stretched over protruding bones. Tattered remnants of what once might have been a miner's uniform clung to its body. The most unsettling feature was its eyes—or the lack thereof. Dark, hollow sockets stared back at them, yet there was an undeniable intelligence, an awareness in its gaze.

Without uttering a word, the figure gestured for them to follow, its humming continuing, echoing through the silent woods. The tune was one of sorrow and longing, but there was also a hint of guidance in it.

Charlotte and Isaac, paralyzed by fear yet feeling an inexplicable trust, began to follow the glowing lantern. The path they treated was unfamiliar, yet the Zombie Miner led them with confidence, manoeuvring around pitfalls and dense underbrush.

Hours seemed to pass, the trio moving in a silent procession. Just when Charlotte felt she couldn't go on any longer, the unmistakable outline of the main road appeared. The Zombie Miner halted at the forest's edge, pointing them towards the safety of the paved path.

Turning to thank their unlikely saviour, Charlotte gasped. The figure had vanished, the lantern's glow extinguished, leaving them in the soft moonlight.

Overwhelmed with a mix of relief and terror, the couple made their way back to their car, the events of the night replaying in their minds. They later learned from locals about the legend of the Zombie Miner, a spirit doomed to wander Cannock Chase, forever seeking the exit from the mine that had been his untimely grave. Yet, over the years, he had morphed from a figure of terror to a guardian of the lost, his lantern becoming a beacon for those who strayed too far from safety.

Charlotte and Isaac ventured into those woods again only once, but they would always remember the night they were saved by the guiding glow of the Zombie Miner. The mournful tune he hummed remained etched in their memories, a chilling reminder of the thin line between the world of the living and the realm of the supernatural.

Zombie in the Town Centre

Cannock, a quaint town that seamlessly merged the hustle and bustle of modern living with the serenity of its historical roots. By day, the town centre was a hub of activities, filled with shoppers, tourists, and locals going about their day. But at night, especially on weekends, the atmosphere shifted. Pubs and bars became lively, drawing in youth from the surrounding areas.

One such Sunday morning in September, at a time when most of Cannock was lost to slumber, two teenagers, Grace and Toby, found themselves wandering the streets. The two had been at a friend's house party, and losing track of time, decided it was best to head home rather than crash there. Their slightly inebriated state lent a soft focus to the world, and Cannock's streets, normally so familiar, felt oddly new and mysterious.

It was 3 am. The streets were eerily silent save for the occasional gust of wind rustling the leaves. Streetlights stood like solitary sentinels, casting long and unpredictable shadows that seemed to play tricks on the eyes.

Toby, ever the prankster, made ghostly noises, trying to spook Grace. She responded with a playful shove. "Knock it off, Tob. This place is creepy enough without you adding to it."

They laughed it off, continuing their trek home, weaving through the streets. As they approached the heart of the town centre, however, their playful banter ceased. A strange echoing sound came from behind them, faint at first but growing louder with each step.

They both turned around, squinting against the low light. To their horror, they discerned the figure of a man emerging from a narrow alley next to The Merchant pub. He was covered in grime and dirt, and his attire looked dated, as though he'd stepped out from another era. His face was barely visible, obscured by shadows and the filth that seemed to cling to him. But the hollow, vacant look in his eyes was unmistakable.

Fear gripped the two friends instantly. The eerie silence of the town centre was disrupted by the heavy, ragged breathing of this figure, echoing strangely as if emanating from the depths of abandoned mines. Every time they took a step back, the figure advanced two. Soon, they realised this wasn't just some drunk or homeless man lost in the town. The way he moved, the unsettling pace at which he approached them—it wasn't natural.

Without uttering a word to each other, both Grace and Toby began to run. They bolted, the only sound being the rapid pounding of their hearts and the echoing footsteps of their pursuer. Every turn they took, they hoped would distance them from the relentless entity behind. But no matter how fast or far they seemed to run, the echoing footsteps maintained their haunting rhythm.

As they sprinted past the old clock tower, Toby chanced a look back. The figure was closer than ever, his arms outstretched, reaching for them with hands that looked mangled and decayed. His face, visible now in the intermittent streetlights, was a ghastly shade of grey, eyes hollowed, and mouth open in a grotesque grimace. There was no breath, no sign of life, only the relentless pursuit.

In a desperate bid to escape, Grace and Toby ran into the stairway for the multi-storey car park. The two pressed themselves against the wall, their breaths shallow and rapid. They hoped their pursuer might walk past, that he might lose track of them.

But hope is a fragile thing in the dead of night.

From the entrance of the stairwell, the echoing footsteps grew louder. The grimy, zombie-like miner entered, his vacant gaze locking onto theirs. In this tight space, his presence was even more intimidating, every detail of his decayed state glaringly visible.

Toby, thinking on his feet, picked up an old discarded bottle and hurled it towards the monster. The sudden impact caught the zombie miner by surprise, and for a split second, he seemed disoriented. That moment was all the teenagers needed. With adrenaline coursing through their veins, they sprinted past the confused entity, back onto the streets.

The chase resumed, but this time, the friends had a plan. Leading the miner towards the more populated areas, they hoped the presence of others might deter him, or at least that they'd find a police officer on patrol.

As they neared the White Hart pub, its lights still on from the previous night's party, they banged on the windows, screamed for help. The owner, shocked by the sight of two terrified teenagers, quickly let them in.

Locking the door behind them, they watched through the glass as the miner approached. But as he neared the pub, he seemed to grow hesitant. He stopped, his hollow eyes scanning the building, and then, with an almost frustrated air, he turned and disappeared into the night.

Safe within the confines of the pub, Grace and Toby tried to recount their harrowing experience to the bewildered owner. But words failed them; how could they explain the sheer terror of being pursued by something not of this world?

The incident that night became one of many whispered tales among the residents of Cannock. The streets of the town centre, while bustling during the day, would forever hold a shadow of fear for Grace and Toby. And though they never encountered the zombie miner again, his echoing footsteps haunted their dreams for years to come.

Four Ashes' Fading Farewell

2003, a year not particularly distinguished in the annals of Cannock's history. Yet, close to Four Ashes, an unremarkable event would unravel an eerie tale that would unsettle the town's residents for years to come.

Rachel, a young historian with a penchant for exploring abandoned structures, chanced upon a dilapidated hut on the outskirts of Four Ashes. Overgrown with ivy and other creepers, the hut was hardly visible to the casual observer. However, Rachel's trained eyes saw past nature's camouflage. Drawn to the hut, she dreamed it would be possible to find trinkets, photographs, or written records that could provide a window into the past.

Pushing open the rickety door, she was met with a musty smell that spoke of years of neglect. The floorboards creaked under her weight, and dust clouds rose in protest to her intrusion. Amidst the decay, Rachel's eyes were drawn to an old leather-bound diary resting on a wooden table, its pages yellowed with age.

Opening the diary, she was met with neat cursive writing. The diary belonged to a miner named Samuel. The entries chronicled the mundane aspects of life—his work in the mines, his hopes, his family, and his friends. However, as Rachel flipped through the pages, a series of entries caught her attention.

"June 8th: Every dawn, as I make my way to work, I see him. At the edge of the clearing, close to the hut. He just stands there, watching, before fading away with the first rays of the sun."

"June 15th: It's been a week now. Like clockwork, he's there. I tried approaching him today, but he vanished before I could get close. It's unsettling."

"June 20th: I've noticed he always looks towards the mine. It's as if he's mourning or searching for something or someone."

"June 25th: Today, he was closer to the hut. For the first time, I saw his face clearly. Grey, hollow eyes that held an ocean of sorrow. Decaying hands that reached out to the mine. Is he a spectre from a mining accident? Or is my mind playing tricks on me?"

"July 1st: He's real. I'm certain. Today, I waited for him. As dawn broke, he appeared. I mustered the courage to call out to him. No response. But as he began to fade, I swear he looked straight at me. Those eyes... They'll haunt me."

The diary entries stopped after that. The pages that followed were blank, leaving Rachel with a chilling mystery.

Intrigued and apprehensive, she decided to camp out near the hut. As dawn approached the next day, Rachel, wrapped in a blanket and sipping hot tea, positioned herself to watch. The world was quiet, save for the chirping of a few early birds.

The first light of dawn painted the sky in hues of orange and pink. And then, just as Samuel's diary had described, a figure began to materialise near the clearing of the hut. He was dressed as a miner, his attire aged, and his overall appearance spoke of a time long gone. His hollow eyes focused on the distant mine, and an aura of profound sadness seemed to emanate from him.

Frozen in her spot, Rachel's heart raced. The diary had been accurate. This wasn't a legend or a figment of a tired miner's imagination. She was witnessing the spectral figure of the Zombie Miner. As the sun's rays grew stronger, the figure began to fade, his last gaze fixed upon the mine he seemingly loved or perhaps mourned.

Sleep eluded Rachel that night. The very ground she stood on, the history of the place, had taken a different, haunting hue. The diary had provided a first-hand account, but witnessing the apparition added a visceral dimension to the story.

Word spread about Rachel's experience and some locals began to visit the hut at dawn, hoping for a glimpse of the mysterious figure. And more often than you'd believe, they were rewarded. The miner was consistent, his routine unaltered. Always appearing at dawn, he gazed longingly towards the mine and vanished with the first strong rays of the sun.

For the residents of Cannock, the Zombie Miner has become a symbol of the town's deep-rooted connection to its mining history. While some found the tale romantic, a testament to the miner's dedication to his work, others found it deeply unsettling—a reminder that there were stories and souls that remained anchored to the land long after they were gone.

Yet, with time, as all tales do, these particular sightings of the Zombie Miner began to fade. Perhaps it was because the sightings became less frequent or because newer generations were less connected to the mining history of Cannock. However, those who had read Samuel's diary or witnessed the apparition knew that somewhere close to Four Ashes, a lost soul still wandered, silently saying his goodbyes to the land he once worked.

Afterword

As I close the pages of this collection, recounting the haunting presence of the Zombie Miner of Cannock Chase, I am once again reminded of the complex tapestry of history, folklore, human psychology, and possibly, the unexplained. Each tale, every encounter, draws us deeper into a mystery that has, over the years, become a profound part of the local consciousness.

It is crucial to approach these accounts with an open mind, and also with a certain level of scepticism. Over the decades, the region's deep-rooted mining history, coupled with genuine tragedy and loss, has given birth to countless stories. These tales could be a manifestation of collective grief, a society's way of remembering and honouring the hardworking souls who once delved into the earth. It is not uncommon for places with rich histories to manifest tales of spirits and apparitions, especially when intertwined with genuine emotion and pain.

There are also the natural phenomena to consider. The mists, the echoes in the woods, the manner in which sound travels, or even the moonlight casting eerie shadows—all of these can play tricks on the mind, especially when one is already steeped in local lore. Our human minds are hardwired to find patterns and familiar shapes, even where none exist, a phenomenon known as pareidolia. Could the sightings of the Zombie Miner be a result of this? It's a possibility.

Yet, while science and psychology offer explanations, they cannot account for every account in this book. There are tales here which defy logical explanation—like the harmonising melodies at Leacroft or the guiding lantern light near Gentleshaw. These are tales that have been recounted by multiple, unrelated individuals who all share an eerily similar narrative.

There is also another perspective to consider: the culture. Mythology and folklore often spring from a society's need to explain the unexplainable, to make sense of things beyond their understanding. The Zombie Miner, in many ways, is a symbol of Cannock Chase's past—a testament to its deep mining roots. He is a tragic figure, caught between worlds, but he is also a protector, a guardian of the land and its people.

In my years as a paranormal investigator, I have come to understand that truth, especially when it pertains to the supernatural, is multifaceted. It's never just black or white. Perhaps there is a real entity that roams Cannock Chase, tethered to the land due to some unfinished business or deep-seated emotion. Or maybe, the Zombie Miner is an embodiment of the region's collective memory—a spectral figure arising from stories passed down through generations, becoming more tangible with every telling.

Whatever the case, the tales of the Zombie Miner of Cannock Chase are a testament to the region's rich history, its people, and the mysteries that life often presents us with. Whether you choose to believe or remain sceptical, one thing is certain: the tales within these pages speak of something profound, something that touches the very core of our understanding of life, death, and everything in between.

Until our paths cross again in another mysterious journey, I leave you with a quote that often guides my investigations: "The boundaries which divide Life from Death are at best shadowy and vague. Who shall say where the one ends, and where the other begins?" - Edgar Allan Poe.

Yours in curiosity,

Lee Brickley.

About the Author

Lee Brickley is an investigator and author with more than 30 titles currently in publication covering a broad range of subjects including true crime, ancient history, the paranormal, and more.

Born in England, Brickley has been a professional writer for more than two decades. He regularly features in the media due to wide interest in his work, and he has made numerous TV appearances.

For more books by this author, simply search "Lee Brickley" on Amazon.

Printed in Great Britain
by Amazon